Kinds of Coins

Learning the Values of Pennies, Nickels, Dimes, and Quarters

Victoria Braidich

New York

We use money to buy things.

Coins are one kind of money.

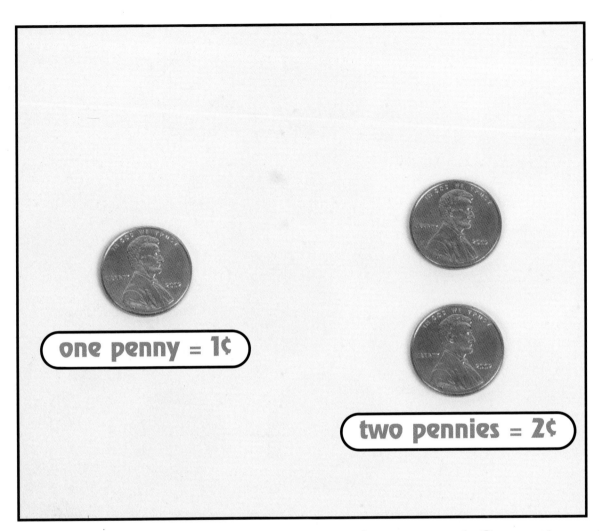

one penny = 1¢

two pennies = 2¢

A penny is 1 cent. Two pennies equal 2 cents.

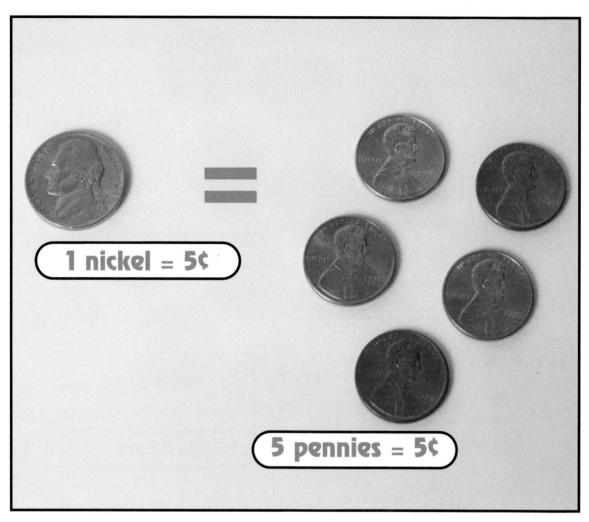

1 nickel = 5¢

5 pennies = 5¢

A nickel is 5 cents. One nickel equals 5 pennies.

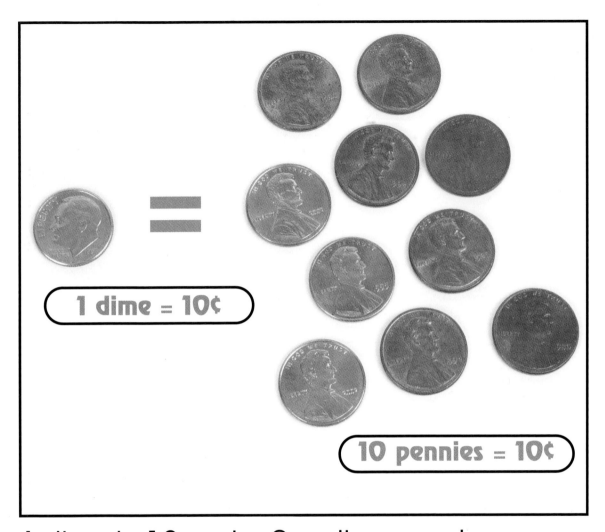

1 dime = 10¢

10 pennies = 10¢

A dime is 10 cents. One dime equals
10 pennies.

One dime also equals 2 nickels.

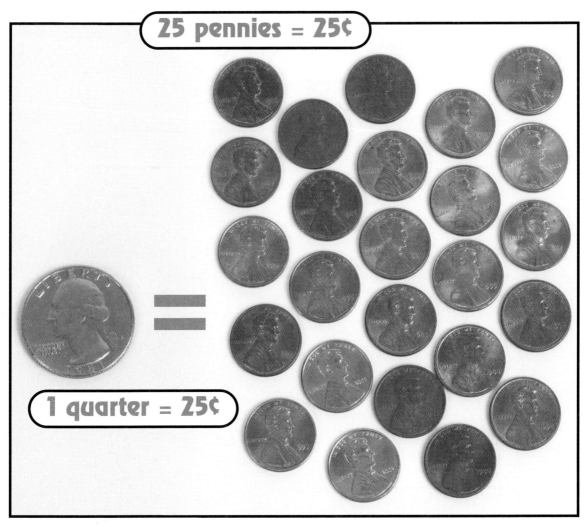

One quarter is 25 cents. One quarter equals 25 pennies.

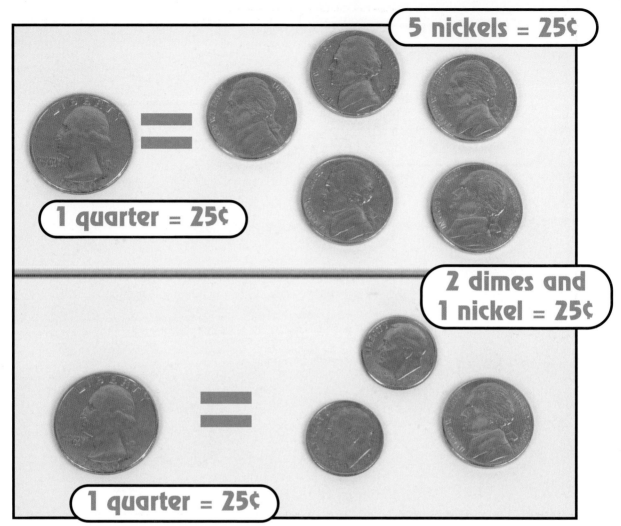

One quarter equals 5 nickels. One quarter also equals 2 dimes and 1 nickel.

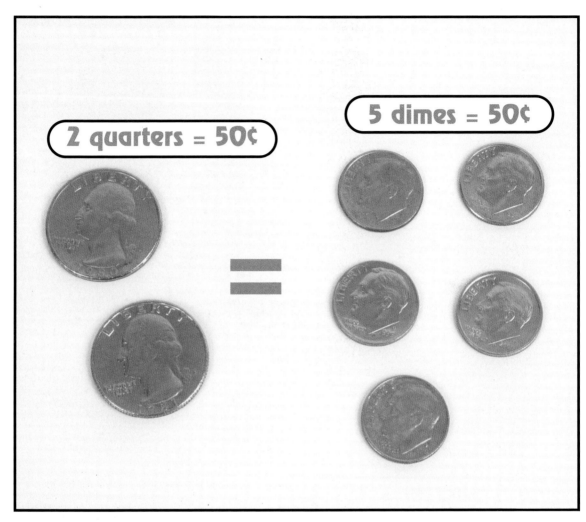

Two quarters are 50 cents. Two quarters equal 5 dimes.

What are some other ways to make 50 cents with pennies, nickels, dimes, and quarters?

Words to Know

coins

dime

equal

nickel

penny

quarter